Impressions of Historic Fredericton

IMPRESSIONS OF HISTORIC FREDERICTON

Paintings by
FERNANDO POYATOS

Text by WILLIAM SPRAY

The painter and the writer would like to express their gratitude to the staff of Goose Lane Editions for their advice and assistance in the production of this book.

Cover illustration by Fernando Poyatos.
Cover design by Julie Scriver.
Book design by Julie Scriver and Ryan Astle.
Printed in Canada by Friesens.
10 9 8 7 6 5 4 3 2 1

Canadian Cataloguing in Publication Data

Poyatos, Fernando.
    Impressions of historic Fredericton
    ISBN 0-9683968-0-1

1. Historic buildings — New Brunswick — Fredericton — Pictorial works.
2. Fredericton ((N.B.) — Buildings, structures, etc. — Pictorial works.
I. Spray, W. A.   II. Title

FC2476.7.P69 1998   971.55'515   C98-950177-9
F1044.5.F8P69 1998

Proceeds from the sale of this book will be donated by the artist to the University of New Brunswick Associated Alumni to be used for scholarships for Arts students attending the University of New Brunswick.

Produced by Goose Lane Editions for Fernando Poyatos and William Spray.

Table of Contents

Public Buildings

REFACE

Fredericton — New Brunswick's "Noble Daughter of the Forest" — is blessed with beauty, history, and heritage, and is lovingly painted by Professor Fernando Poyatos.

This spectacular collection of artwork, commemorating the City of Fredericton's hundred and fiftieth anniversary of incorporation, mirrors what our city once was, is today, and always will be.

Fernando Poyatos has successfully captured the true essence of Fredericton. His love for this city is as vivid as his portrayals of splendid Victorian architecture, the vibrant hues of which genuinely reflect the warmth of our people, regardless of the season.

I hope you will enjoy this exceptional collection as much as I have, and that *Impressions of Historic Fredericton* will become a keepsake to be cherished and appreciated by generations to come.

Brad Woodside
Mayor

Acknowledgements

The painter and the author are very grateful to Bob Skillen, who believed in this book and who, through initiative and tireless effort, made *Impressions of Historic Fredericton* a financially viable project. They particularly thank the University of New Brunswick Associated Alumni for its generous assistance, and they gratefully acknowledge the support of the following patrons:

ADI Group Inc.

Michael Bardsley/ Nesbitt Burns

Bird Holdings Ltd.

Greg Byrne, MLA, Minister of Justice
and Attorney General, Province of
New Brunswick

City of Fredericton

Wilma and John Clark

Marilyn Trenholme Counsell,
Lieutenant-Governor,
Province of New Brunswick

Ivan H. Crowell

Greenarm Management Ltd.

Fredericton Foundation

Fredericton Heritage Trust

Mary Dingee Jacobs and Paul Jacobs

Margaret and William Jones

Kileel Developments Ltd.

Colin B. Mackay, President Emeritus,
University of New Brunswick

Tony Mais

Joanne and Reid Manore

NB Power Corp.

NB Tel

Neill and Gunter Ltd.

Elizabeth Parr-Johnston, President,
University of New Brunswick

Ross Ventures Ltd.

Royal Bank Financial Group

ScotiaMcLeod

Andy Scott, M.P., Solicitor General of
Canada

Janet and Bob Stevenson

University of New Brunswick Bookstore

University of New Brunswick
Faculty of Arts

A Personal Tribute

FERNANDO POYATOS

As a newcomer to Fredericton from my native Spain thirty years ago, I soon developed a deep relationship with its architectural and natural environments. My awe and enjoyment compelled me to start sketching and then painting its homes, churches and official and mercantile buildings as a means of gratefully expressing my close interaction with them. As a medium I chose mostly the water-based pigment known as gouache, which often I use straight from the tube, even with only my palette knife, to create certain textures.

I hope that your eyes will feast with me on the charm of this "City of Stately Elms," its intimately articulated buildings pulsating with the lives of those we sense behind their walls and lighted windows. Trees, fences and hedges will whisper in your ear the stories with which my colleague and friend, historian William Spray, has contributed to my portraits of Fredericton. Above all, I think, you will recognize the different moods I so love in the city: hushed under the snow, glittering after a spring shower, cuddled in the warm brightness and fragrance of a summer morning, romantically enveloped in autumnal colours or in the subdued greys and greens of a quiet overcast weekend. You will relive with me its quiet evenings, the creaking of its old floors and stairs, its crows cawing in the tree tops or cruising under dramatic skies, the squirrels darting along power cables and leaping between branches, the cooing of pigeons under the eaves of old homes. Light and shadow, sound and silence, movement and stillness, textures and smells, what you see and what you just feel — all have been for me sources of the sensory and aesthetic involvement with which Fredericton has delighted me during the greater part of my life.

Naturally, the city inspired me to paint quite a few other homes and cityscapes not shown here (and others I shall do in the future), which, while being just as characteristic of our town, could not be included in the book for lack of space or because they were not precisely historic. There are two reasons for the preponderance of winter and autumn scenes that some people have pointed out in my work: my personal sensitivity toward the mood in those particular seasons, and the simple fact that my subject matter is hidden from view when the leaves are out.

I wish to pay tribute to this unique city and its people through this long-overdue book. We are about to close a century, and I myself have been a proud witness of Fredericton's growth since I came. And yet I also take pride in the fact that Fredericton remains a privileged place in its persistent quietness, as well as a haven for a tranquil existence which its residents should zealously guard and never take for granted.

My first gratitude is to Fredericton, my forever beautiful model and inexhaustible inspiration. I am very grateful to William Spray, whose eloquence in the text of this book complements my nonverbal portraits of Fredericton. I owe thanks to Mayor Brad Woodside and his Council and to all the other owners of my paintings, who honour me by hanging them in City Hall and in their homes, and who have loaned them for the book-launching exhibition and kindly allowed me to use their names in *Impressions of Historic Fredericton*. I would also like to thank Marie Maltais, Director of the University of New Brunswick Art Centre, and her staff for contributing to the organization of the exhibition, and to the New Brunswick Arts Branch for technical assistance.

Historic Fredericton

WILLIAM SPRAY

This book is an attempt to show the beauty and variety of the buildings which make Fredericton and the surrounding area such an attractive place. Fernando Poyatos has always felt there was something special about many of these buildings, and several years ago he began to paint those which he found artistically interesting and challenging. He also began to ask questions about the buildings. Who constructed them and when? Who lived in them, or what were they used for? In 1994 he asked me to collaborate with him on a book which would include some of his paintings and some information about the buildings.

Finding buildings of historic interest in the Fredericton area was not a very difficult task, but deciding which ones to include in the book was more complicated. The final choice came down to those which had some historical interest or uniqueness and those which best reflected the artist's style and feeling for Fredericton. Many buildings of perhaps equal or greater interest were excluded, but it was impossible to include them all.

The major feature of Fredericton is the beautiful Saint John River and its broad, level plain, which provided a perfect site for a settlement. The earliest settlers of the area were the Native people, the Wolustukwiyik, and their settlement and graveyard were located at St. Anne's Point, near where Government House now stands. In later years the French under Governor Villebon constructed a fort at the mouth of the Nashwaak, and by the 1730s Acadian settlers had established themselves at St. Anne's Point. In 1759 this settlement was destroyed by the English, leaving few European settlers in the area.

The first Loyalists arrived in 1783 and the construction of houses began almost immediately. The town plat was laid out in 1784, the year the province was created, and St. Anne's

Point, now Fredericton, became the provincial capital. Many government buildings were constructed, among them the oldest public building in Fredericton, which stands next to the present Legislature. The city also became the centre for military operations in the province, and some of the old buildings used by the soldiers can still be seen in the Military Compound.

The centre of business activity in the early years was the down-river end of Queen Street and Waterloo Row, where there were a number of inns, a trading post and stores. As the centre of government developed on Queen Street, so did a new active business district, and the down-river area below the government buildings became a residential area for politicians, government officials and prominent businessmen. Farraline Place, once a store and trading post, and the former McLeod's Inn, near the corner of Waterloo Row and University Avenue, are two of the few buildings in this area that have survived from the earlier years.

The first church in Fredericton was a chapel constructed by the Jesuits at St. Anne's Point in the first half of the eighteenth century. By the end of the century the Loyalists had constructed the first Anglican church near the site of the present Christ Church Cathedral. Other religious denominations followed, and their steeples soon dominated the town plat. Fredericton became the site of the first Church of England cathedral built since the Protestant Reformation, and because of this it was often referred to as "the celestial city." It also became the site of King's College, the oldest university building in Canada still in use.

Architecturally and artistically, Fredericton buildings have a fascination for many people and reflect many styles and traditions, from the plain to the very elaborate and ostentatious. Stewart Smith, a former University of New Brunswick art historian, says in the *Heritage Handbook* that the Loyalists introduced Georgian architecture to New Brunswick and the idea of style to building construction. A major change in architectural style took place after the construction of Christ Church Cathedral. In his highly informative book *On Earth as It Is in Heaven: Gothic Revival Churches of Victorian New Brunswick,* Gregg Finley says that Christ Church Cathedral "more than any other single building . . . symbolized the arrival of the Gothic revival in New Brunswick." Gothic Revival was followed by the construction of buildings in imitation of Neo-Grecian, Roman, Italian Renaissance and other architectural styles.

What interests me most is the history of the buildings and the people who lived and worked in them. I find it almost impossible to walk around Fredericton and not be reminded of some part of its history. A visit to St. Anne's Point and Government House evokes images of Wolustukwiyik canoes arriving there in 1763 to inform New England surveyors attempting to lay out a township grant that the land belonged to them. One can imagine an 1840s party at Government House, with its verandas and gardens stretching down to the river, the ladies and gentlemen arriving in fancy gowns, top hats, or full dress military uniforms, while cooks and servants sweated in the kitchens preparing food. One can also imagine Boss Gibson's train pulling out of Marysville and crossing the old railway bridge loaded with mill workers and their families heading off for a picnic.

The face of Fredericton is constantly changing. Walking along King and Queen streets you can admire the few old buildings still standing and study the renovations that keep old structures such as the railway bridge serviceable. It is good to have reminders of what life once was like. Who knows? Perhaps fifty years from now people will stare at what was once a neighbourhood convenience store on some Fredericton corner. They may wonder what it was like to shop in such a place.

The major sources for information used in this book are: *Fredericton, New Brunswick* (Fredericton, 1966), by Isabel Louise Hill; collections of the Provincial Archives of New Brunswick; Dr. Gregg Finley and Lynn Wigginton's *On Earth as It Is in Heaven* (Fredericton: Goose Lane, 1995); Dr. Stewart Smith's "The Architectural History of Fredericton" in *Heritage Handbook* (Fredericton Heritage Trust, 1982) and "Architecture in New Brunswick" in *Canadian Antiques Collector* 10:3 (May-June 1975); various volumes of the *Dictionary of Canadian Biography*; *The Story of Fredericton* (Fredericton, 1980) by W. Austin Squires; *The History of St. Mary's* (1936) by Susan Squires; *The History of Marysville* (Fredericton, 1983) by Douglas Pond; *New Brunswick's Old Government House* (Fredericton: New Ireland, 1994) by George MacBeath; Lilian Maxwell's articles, "A History of Fredericton Gaols," *Maritime Advocate* (November-December 1943) and "Some Historic Buildings of Fredericton, New Brunswick," *Maritime Advocate* (September and October 1953); Ted Jones's, "The Story of Lord and Lady Ashburnham," *Atlantic Advocate* (April and May 1986); Mary Barker's "Period Houses of Fredericton" (New Brunswick Travel Bureau, 1961); numerous articles published in the *Fredericton Daily Gleaner*, in particular those prepared for Fredericton Heritage Trust in the 1970s; *Canada Home* (Vancouver: University of British Columbia, 1983), by Margaret and Thomas Blom; Elizabeth Tucker's *Leaves from Juliana Horatia Ewing's Canada Home* (Boston: Roberts Brothers, 1896); Susan Montague's *A Pictorial History of the University of New Brunswick* (Fredericton, 1992); Glen McIntyre and Bob Watson's, "An Introduction to the Architecture and History of Selected Churches in the Fredericton Area" (Fredericton, 1982); and numerous church histories.

A number of people helped with this research, especially in clarifying facts about certain buildings. I would especially like to thank Marion Beyea, Provincial Archivist; Richard Bird; Edgar Christie; the Rev. David Keirstead; Ronald Miller; Kathy Meagher; Helen Malloy; David Myles; Eric Swanick; and Dr. Murray Young.

HOUSES

Jaffrey House

(63 McKeen Street)

This attractive house was built by William Jaffrey, the son of the Rev. William B. Jaffrey, who was rector of Holy Trinity Church, Lower St. Mary's, from 1851 to 1890. It was built some time after 1878 and was owned by the Jaffrey family until 1949, when it was sold to R.B.Malloy, whose wife Helen still lives there. The widow's walk, unusual for this part of the province, provides a lovely view across the river to downtown Fredericton.

JAFFREY HOUSE

Ingraham House

(306 Brunswick Street)

In 1823 William Mackay sold an acre lot on the corner of Brunswick and Westmorland streets to John and Ira Ingraham of Queensbury. This large, imposing house was built shortly after, probably in 1823 or 1824. It is shown on a map of Fredericton prepared in 1832 as the only house on that block of land. It was sold in 1836 to John A. Beckwith, a prominent businessman and politician, who at various times in later years was the mayor of Fredericton, a member of the Legislative Assembly, the Provincial Secretary, a member of the Executive Council, and finally a member of the Legislative Council. In 1840 he sold the house to J.P.A. Phillips, who became the senior proprietor of the Tory newspaper *Headquarters* when it was first published in 1843. Since that time the house has had numerous owners.

With its cellar kitchen and servants' quarters, this is the house of a well-to-do family. It is very similar in style to the Deanery on Brunswick Street and Farraline Place on Queen Street, although the roof of the Ingraham house has a much steeper pitch, the result of alterations in later years. Its two-storey veranda, beautiful internal staircase and impressive front entrance make it one of the nicest early nineteenth century homes in Fredericton.

INGRAHAM HOUSE

The Deanery

(808 Brunswick Street)

One of the oldest buildings in Fredericton, this house is shown on a 1785 map of the city. At that time it was the residence of the Hon. Jonathan Odell, New Brunswick's first Provincial Secretary. Perhaps the most distinguished Loyalist to come to New Brunswick, Odell was a doctor and minister of the Church of England and had served as Chaplin of the King's American Dragoons. He was also a poet and satirist of note whose verse had served as propaganda for the Loyalist cause.

This house, which was for many years the leading house in Fredericton society, had outbuildings stretching along Church Street from Brunswick to George, all of which have disappeared. The oldest wing, said to be the finest example of pioneer design and construction in New Brunswick, may have been the house built by Philip Weade in 1782. It was a six-room self-contained house with two lofts, one with iron rings, known locally as "the slave rings," bolted to the wall. Odell owned slaves, and similar rings were found in the demolished home of Capt. Stair Agnew, a slave owner who lived on the opposite side of the river before the arrival of the Loyalists.

Philip Weade's land was confiscated in 1785 and regranted to Odell, who built the present house. The Odell family at the time owned about one quarter of what was then Fredericton, including the block below Church Street, half the block above Church, and most of what was then the back of the town. Queen's Square was once the Odells' private park and riding circle. In the study of Odell's house, the officers of the 104th Regiment are said to have planned their historic march to Canada during the War of 1812. After Jonathan Odell's death, his son, William Franklin Odell, occupied the house until 1844. The Hon. S.L. Tilley, a Father of Confederation, leased it for a time in 1867.

In 1910 it passed into the hands of the Bishop and Chapter of the Diocese of Fredericton, and for many years it has been the residence of the Dean of Christ Church Cathedral. This is the most important house in Fredericton because of its influence on subsequent architecture throughout New Brunswick.

THE DEANERY

McLeod's Inn and Bully House

(12-14 Waterloo Row & 10 Waterloo Row)

McLeod's Inn (left) is the only survivor of a series of inns that once existed in Fredericton. It was built sometime after 1786 by Duncan McLeod, who was later a member of the Legislative Assembly. In 1791 McLeod had a tavern license, and in later years he also operated a billiard hall here. In the late eighteenth and early nineteenth centuries, Waterloo Row was a commercial area that included a landing, weigh scales, shops, inns and taverns, and the homes of many tradesmen. Nearby were two other inns, the Golden Ball and the Royal Oak, which, in 1818, advertised "good Entertainment for Man and Horse." Many early visitors to Fredericton stayed at McLeod's Inn, including Patrick Campbell, the author of *Travels in North America*, in 1791. It is unclear when this building ceased to be an inn, but Joseph Gaynor had a store there after 1825. In 1832 Thomas Pickard purchased the building, and his son-in-law, Oliver Smith, also had a store there for some time. In 1859 it became the residence of George Priestly, barrack master at the Fredericton garrison. His daughter married Charles Watters, who was active in government from 1846 to 1867. In 1870 Watters was appointed a judge of the Court of Common Pleas in Saint John, and he and his wife later sold the property to Arthur Bully, a carpenter. Bully also owned a new house which he had constructed next door. He is supposed to have made alterations to the old inn between 1878 and 1880, including the removal of the large middle chimney, which he replaced with several smaller chimneys. This may have been when the inn was made into a duplex and it and the Bully house joined together. William Watson, a politician and County Court judge, bought the two buildings in 1880 and lived there for about forty years. Today both buildings have been divided into apartments.

McLeod's Inn and Bully House

Farraline Place

(776 Queen Street)

Peter Fraser, a successful fur trader who came to New Brunswick from Scotland in 1784, built this large residence, which he called Cambourne House, in 1791. He lived in the down-river end of the building and operated a trading post or store in the upper end. Described as "the greatest buyer and exporter of peltry in New Brunswick," he also dealt in lumber and supplied all sorts of goods to lumber-men. His store had an ideal location, since there were two boat landings nearby, and he had a window cut in the room above the store so he could view all upriver traffic as well as the sunset over the river. He became a colonel in the militia and was a member of the Legislative Assembly from 1809 until 1827. He was the first president of the Fredericton Society of St. Andrews (1825-1832), and he became vice-president of the Bank of New Brunswick in 1832 and vice-president of the Fredericton Savings Bank in 1835.

In later years the house was owned by the Hon. Peter Minchin, a member of the Executive Council, and from 1876 to 1893 a Mrs. Tippet, the widow of an Anglican clergyman, lived here. The Hon. James Fraser, a former premier, bought the house in 1894 after he became lieutenant-governor; he was the first lieutenant-governor not to be provided with an official residence owned by the province. He renamed the house Farraline Place. Lieutenant-Governor Fraser died in 1896, and his wife lived in the house until her death in 1907. In her will she left the building and an endowment to maintain it as a home for elderly women. In 1920 the house was turned over to the New Brunswick branch of the King's Daughters and Sons as the J.J. Fraser Farraline Place, and it was formally opened on 25 January 1921. It could accommodate ten guests; in the next ten years twenty-one elderly persons entered the home, where, as reported in the *Daily Gleaner* on 29 January 1931, they "enjoyed comfort and happiness in their declining years." Twelve residents were said to "have been called to their Eternal Home." The side porch, dormer windows and overmantles of the windows were added in the late nineteenth century.

FARRALINE PLACE

Gill House

(968 Riverside Drive, Lower St. Marys)

There are two old stone houses located on the north side of the Saint John River below the Princess Margaret Bridge. One is the Gill House, which for 134 years belonged to a family of successful farmers, stone masons, mill owners, teachers and proprietors of the Gibson and Douglas ferries. Ensign Thomas Gill of the Maryland Loyalists was aboard the transport *Martha*, which was shipwrecked off the coast of Nova Scotia in 1783. Over a hundred died in the wreck, including, according to family tradition, Gill's wife and child. He remarried shortly afterwards, and in 1784 he was given a grant of 550 acres in the block of land reserved for the Maryland Loyalists in Lower St. Marys. He first built a log house, which was replaced in 1788 by this small house of Georgian design, fronting on the river, with a central door flanked by two windows on each side and five windows across the second storey. It was constructed primarily of field stone, and large stone arches in the basement supported the chimneys. Some people believed these arches to be the remains of an old French powder magazine thought to have been situated here, but there is no evidence to support this claim.

In the 1840s a small wooden addition was added to the building, and changes were made to accommodate the highway which had been constructed behind the house. The Gill family occupied the house until 1922, when it was acquired by the Soldiers' Settlement Board. It was later owned by Samuel Lean, who demolished the 1840s addition in the 1930s and added a new one. This addition was replaced in 1973 with one more in keeping with the 1788 house, which is at present owned by Richard Bird.

GILL HOUSE

Peppers House

(10 Stone House Lane, Lower St. Marys)

The date of the construction of the Peppers House, the second of the old stone houses still standing in Lower St. Marys, is uncertain. It was built of local stone on land granted in 1784 to Levin Townsend, a Loyalist, and it was there in 1788 when the land was leased to John Montford and William Anderson. William was the son of John Anderson, who had established a trading post at the mouth of the Nashwaak River in 1763, and he eventually became owner of the property. In 1811, after William's death, a portion of the lot containing the stone house was sold to Edward Winslow Miller. In 1833 he sold it to Col. Thomas Peppers, who had served in the British Army and had come to New Brunswick with the 81st Regiment in 1820. Col. Peppers had begun buying land near Baillie's Ferry in Lower St. Marys in 1828. By 1833 he owned 825 acres including the stone house. It is very strongly built, with walls two feet thick and corners made of stones fitted together log cabin-style. The doors and window casements are ornamented with brick, and the windows have inside shutters which could be locked. Col. Peppers farmed his land until his death in 1847, and his family continued to occupy the land until 1984. It is now owned by Owen and Valerie Fowler.

PEPPERS HOUSE

EDGECOMBE HOUSE

(736 King Street)

This very elaborate house, with its towers, cupolas and bay windows, was originally constructed as a simple five-bayed house very similar to the Deanery. It was built in the early 1800s for Henry Smith, a Loyalist who purchased the property in 1807. When Government House was destroyed by fire in 1825, Smith, who was having financial problems, rented his house to the government as a residence for Lieutenant-Governor Sir Howard Douglas while a new Government House was being constructed on Woodstock Road. The government spent considerable money to renovate the building and purchase furniture for a Council Chamber set up in a second house nearby, which was also rented from Smith.

The first big event in the new government residence was the celebration of the King's birthday. The actual birthday was on a Sunday, but the celebrations were postponed until Tuesday 25 April, 1826. After a big parade, "His Excellency gave an elegant Dinner to as many Gentlemen as could be accommodated in his present residence; the hilarity and good humour of which was much heightened by the attention and affability of Sir Howard and his amiable Lady, and the whole company entered into the true spirit of the day, and His Majesty's health was drank with the most enthusiastic loyalty, accompanied with God save the King, by the band of the 52nd Regiment."

After Sir Howard moved into the newly constructed Government House in 1828, Smith sold the house to Charles S. Putnam, Clerk of the Supreme Court and grandson of the Hon. James Putnam, a former judge of the Supreme Court, who began to call the building Willow House. It was occupied for thirty years by Chief Justice Sir John Allen, an opponent of Confederation, who became Chief Justice of the province in 1865. In the late 1880s it was purchased by Frederick B. Edgecombe, at that time Fredericton's most successful dry goods merchant and largest real estate owner, who was responsible for all the alterations. He added towers and cupolas, bay widows and verandas, and the result is what you see now: a mixture of so many architectural styles that it is no longer possible to recognise the original simple five-bayed house so common in late eighteenth- and early nineteenth-century New Brunswick.

EDGECOMBE HOUSE

Saunders House

(752 King Street)

Next to the Edgecombe House is a much more modest building constructed by a very prominent Virginia Loyalist, the Hon. John Saunders. Built in 1795 or 1796, it is one of the few surviving Loyalist homes in Fredericton. The front entrance, fan lights and side lights are early nineteenth century additions. Side gables and a veranda were added later in the century, but the veranda has since been removed. Saunders had been a captain in the Queen's Rangers and had fought bravely in a number of major battles during the American Revolutionary War. After the war ended he spent some time in England and was called to the bar in 1787. In 1790 he was appointed one of the judges of the Supreme Court of New Brunswick, the only opponent of slavery on the bench at that time. He was also the only judge of the Supreme Court ever to hold a seat in the Legislative Assembly at the same time.

This modest house or cottage, with its basement kitchen and wine cellar, was for a time the town residence of Judge Saunders. When needed at court he would arrive here in his yellow coach from his principal residence, the Barony, near the mouth of Pokiok Stream, about forty miles upriver from Fredericton, where he was attempting to recreate his Virginia estates on the banks of the Saint John River. For a time the Barony was the largest estate in the province; Thomas Baillie, Commissioner of Crown Lands, claimed it contained 9000 acres.

After Saunders died, much of the land reverted to wilderness, and much of it remains unoccupied. Judge Saunders also owned a number of other properties in Fredericton, and it is not clear how long he used his cottage. In 1826, he sold it to Joseph Gaynor, a merchant, and it was occupied for a time by one of his relatives, Catherine Dayton, who, along with her mother, had a school there. Robert Gowan, a banker, journalist and civil servant, purchased the house in 1836. After his death in 1879, it was bought by Robert Macredie and was occupied by his descendants until 1987. It is now owned by David Myles.

SAUNDERS HOUSE (752 KING STREET)

Saunders House

(177 University Avenue)

Built for Chief Justice John Saunders, this house was "erected to be a monument" to those who had established Fredericton as New Brunswick's capital. The province's first Government House was one of the buildings partially destroyed by a major fire in 1825. Judge Saunders salvaged as much of the building as possible and had it carted down to his land on the corner of Brunswick Street and University Avenue. He used some of this material in the construction of this new house, including all of the woodwork from the old dining room, where he had "enjoyed many a glass of wine to 'King and Country' with men famous in the early history of this country." The exact date of construction is not certain, but it was finished before Saunders died in 1834. For a time the house was occupied by the Hon. James Carter, a newly appointed judge of the Supreme Court, who arrived in 1836. Judge Saunders's wife died in 1845 and his estate was divided. A grandson, John Saunders Flood, then became the owner of this house. A year later, in 1846, Judge Carter purchased Frogmore, than an estate and now 535 Beaverbrook Street, and around the same time Flood sold the house to Charlotte Murray, the daughter of Stair Agnew, a prominent Loyalist and former member of the Executive Council. Since that time the house has had a number of owners, many of whom were connected in one way or another with government, including William McLean, High Sheriff of York County; James Steadman, Postmaster General, 1860-1865; and Theodore Barker, who was for many years secretary to the lieutenant-governors of the province.

Saunders House (177 University Avenue)

Sunbury Cottage

(120 University Avenue)

This house was built in 1830 by Andrew Richey, a twenty-year-old Irishman who arrived in Fredericton in 1828. It was constructed on the back part of a large lot extending from Waterloo Row to Sunbury Street (now University Avenue) which was owned by his mother-in-law, the widow of William Anderson. At the time Richey was employed as a carpenter on the construction of a tannery on the next lot. In 1834 he purchased the portion of the lot on which his house stood from his mother-in-law for five shillings. The house is very solidly built. It is thought to have been constructed in stages, beginning with a cellar paved with stones approximately three feet across and with walls three feet thick, a single room above at street level and a small upper chamber reached by a steep stairway. The larger portion of the house was added later to make this one of the prettiest old homes in Fredericton. The Richey family continued to occupy the house for approximately one hundred years. Andrew's son Marshall became president of the Fredericton Gas Works, which brought the first gas lights to Fredericton's streets. The house was sold by the family in 1926, but in 1963 it was purchased by a great-great-granddaughter of Andrew Richey, Mrs. D.L. Forbes, who still resides there.

SUNBURY COTTAGE

COURTESY OF PATRICIA FORBES

ELMONT

(Lincoln)

This beautifully proportioned old house, almost two hundred years old, stands in an apple orchard in Lincoln, nine miles below Fredericton. Five wide windows stretch across the second storey and two half-moon windows light the attic at the north and south sides. Built of yellow pine and put together with hand-wrought nails, it has been called an "inside-out house," since it is wood on the outside but is lined throughout with brick to make it frostproof in winter and cool in summer.

Although Belmont is most closely associated with the Wilmot family, the land was originally purchased in 1785 by Daniel Bliss, a Loyalist and a member of the governor's council. His son, the Hon. John Murray Bliss, who later became a judge of the Supreme Court, supposedly moved there in 1816. By 1820 he had either rebuilt a house already on the property or constructed a new one, which was said to be the "most stately dwelling of that time on the Saint John River." The judge rode to Fredericton in a fine coach with outriders, and for many years the house was the scene of numerous social events.

Judge Bliss died in 1834. His sister Hannah had married William Wilmot, who owned the adjoining estate, and in 1839 Belmont passed into the hands of the Wilmot family. The Hon. Robert Duncan Wilmot resided there from 1851 until his death in 1891, except for his term as lieutenant-governor, when he occupied Government House. A prominent government figure for many years, his offices included surveyor general, provincial secretary, speaker of the senate and lieutenant-governor of the province, and he was also a Father of Confederation.

Belmont is reputed to have its own resident ghost or ghosts that haunt the stairwells and upper rooms. According to those who have lived there, it is common to hear sharp sounds, doors opening and closing, and feet clattering about, but to see no sign of life. Occasionally a lady in grey is observed on the staircase. A descendant of the Wilmot family claimed many years ago that the ghost might be an ancestor who committed suicide there.

BELMONT

FROGMORE

(535 Beaverbrook Street)

This huge house stands on part of the seventy-two acre estate granted to George Sproule, a Loyalist who was New Brunswick's first surveyor general. This estate stretched along the Maryland Hill (now Regent Street) from George Street north to Montgomery Street. Sproule died in 1817, and in 1822 his executors sold eleven acres of the estate, including a house, barns and fences, to James Holbrook, a teacher at the Fredericton Collegiate School. Holbrook added a wing to the house before he sold the property in 1846 to the Hon. James Carter, who became Chief Justice of New Brunswick. In 1865, Carter retired from the bench, and he returned to England in 1866. Before he left, he sold his estate to Archibald Drummond Fitz Randolph, a prominent merchant, who was for a time a member of the Legislative Council. Randolph expanded the estate in 1871 by purchasing the adjoining eight acres, and he added beautiful gardens, ornamental flower beds, hedges and gravel walks. He called the estate Frogmore, perhaps naming it after Queen Victoria's beloved estate at Windsor, or perhaps in humorous recognition of the large pond below the house which was a home to many frogs. Archibald Randolph moved to California in 1896, and his son Alan lived at Frogmore until 1922.

A number of renovations were made to the house in the early years of this century, including the removal of the bell pulls scattered throughout the house to summon the servants. A large bell which had hung at the back of the house to call the field workers also disappeared. After Ashley Coulter bought Frogmore in 1922, he sold the old coach house, which had been part of every gentleman's estate in the days of horses and buggies, and it was moved to Albert Street and converted into a house.

The old gate house was moved from near Regent Street to Beaverbrook Street, enlarged and rented; it was recently demolished. Historian Dr. Murray Young, who once lived in this house, claims that it also housed a ghost. James Ross, a Fredericton businessman and former senator, lived in Frogmore for fifteen years, and he remains its owner.

Frogmore

Beechmount

(621 Regent Street)

Originally part of the Sproule estate, Beechmount, a property of about twenty-eight acres, was sold to the Hon. George Frederick Street, who went to live there in 1834. Street had gained considerable notoriety in 1821 when he killed another prominent Fredericton lawyer, George L. Wetmore, in a duel. Street and his second fled to the United States; on their return they were tried for murder but acquitted. Street went on to become solicitor general and later a judge of the Supreme Court. When he died in 1856, Beechmount was sold to Dr. Hiram Dow, the best known medical practitioner in the city. He was one of the first to use chloroform in his operations, which were frequently reported in the newspapers. Dow was also a dentist and the inventor of Dr. Dow's Sturgeon Oil Liniment, a popular remedy which some felt would result in the disappearance of sturgeon from the Saint John river. A year after he purchased Beechmount, a fire destroyed the outbuildings, and a week later a second fire destroyed the original house. Both fires were said to have been deliberately set. Dow did not rebuild but instead sold the estate in 1858 to Christopher Broderick, a butcher, who built the present house. The estate had several owners before it passed into the hands of Henry Phair in 1874. Phair was a prominent barrister who "sang pleasant, was good company, made delightful etchings and other pictures, and was a keen sportsman." He is said to have accompanied President Theodore Roosevelt on his fishing trips to New Brunswick. Nathan C. Squires purchased the estate in 1897, and the Squires family has occupied the house since that time. For many years it was the home of Dr. W. Austin Squires, a biologist and authority on ornithology as well as the author of several books on New Brunswick history, including a history of Fredericton.

Fernando Poyatos/97

BEECHMOUNT

ELMCROFT

(9 Elmcroft Place)

Elmcroft was built on a ten-acre lot off Waterloo Row that included the first Loyalist encampment and a small burial ground containing the graves of Loyalists who died during the winter of 1783-1784, their first winter at St. Anne's Point. The lot was granted to Philip Weade, one of the first English-speaking settlers in the area. Whether or not he had a house on this lot is uncertain. The land was acquired by Henry Smith in 1797, and he may have been responsible for the construction of the spacious two-storey house, "having four good Rooms on the first flat, six Bed Rooms on the second flat, five good Rooms in the Garrett, and four Rooms in the Cellar, lathed and plastered," which was purchased in 1839 by the Hon. Neville Parker, a prominent barrister who later became a judge.

In 1865 Parker sold the house to George Clopper Ketchum, who just three years earlier had received the first diploma in civil engineering awarded by the University of New Brunswick. Ketchum was involved in the construction of the Sao Paulo Railway in Brazil as well as railways in New Brunswick, but he is chiefly remembered for his attempt to construct a railway to carry ships across the Isthmus of Chignecto, a project that ended in failure when the federal government withdrew its support in 1891. Ketchum added a full third storey to the house for a billiard room, which he topped with a mansard roof.

The property was famous for its conservatory and beautiful gardens, and Ketchum paid for the planting of trees along Waterloo Row as well as the oaks still standing in front of the house. His wife was one of Fredericton's leading hostesses, and the house was the scene of many fancy dress balls. Frequent visitors to the Ketchum home were Dr. George Parkin, the principal of the Fredericton Collegiate School, and the young writers Charles G.D. Roberts, Bliss Carman and Francis Sherman.

ELMCROFT

41

Taylor House

(232 Northumberland Street)

George T. Taylor was one of New Brunswick's most famous early photographers and a pioneer in nature photography. He was born in 1838, and in 1846 he moved with his family to this house, which was constructed by his father, William Taylor, a carpenter. The Taylor family continued to reside here for over one hundred and thirty years.

George Taylor began his photographic career in 1856, when he built his first camera out of wood and produced his first daguerreotypes. He built every camera he ever used and became very skilled in the wet plate process, which he learned from David Lawrence, a Fredericton portrait photographer. In 1861 Taylor composed the first panoramic photograph of Fredericton. A personal friend of the Hon. Arthur Hamilton Gordon, who was lieutenant-governor of New Brunswick from 1861 to 1866, Taylor frequently visited Government House and was the first to photograph it.

In 1863 Gordon requested that Taylor travel about the province taking photographic views, and he gave Taylor a letter requesting that people assist him as best they could. Taylor took hundreds of photographs of mills, lumber camps, steam boats, military manoeuvres, and religious and educational buildings, continuing this fieldwork until 1906. Some of his work was published in *The Canadian Illustrated News* in 1871-1872.

An excellent portrait photographer, he took portraits of many prominent people, including Lieutenant-Governor Sir Leonard Tilley and his wife and the Rev. Dr. George Goodridge Roberts. Although Taylor died in 1913, his photographs are often used as illustrations in books on New Brunswick history. He was also a talented artist, and his paintings are much sought after today.

Taylor House

*A*SHBURNHAM *H*OUSE
(163-165 Brunswick Street)

The Ashburnham House was originally two buildings, one an old inn and the other the residence of William Anderson, a city alderman. The most famous occupants of this building were Maria "Rye" Anderson and Thomas Ashburnham, the youngest son of Lord Ashburnham, the head of one of the most ancient families in England and owner of one of the loveliest properties there. As a fifth son, there was no expectation that Thomas would ever assume the title; he spent twenty six years in the army and was decorated for bravery. The family then sent him out to Canada, and he arrived in Fredericton as a typical remittance man, living on an allowance provided by the family.

Here Thomas fell in love with Rye Anderson, a telephone operator, and they were married in June, 1903. Ashburnham had already purchased the two houses on Brunswick Street, and the two buildings were joined by a glassed-in conservatory forming a *porte cochére* which provided access to the back of the house and Ashburnham's beautiful lawns and gardens. Thomas resided in one house and his wife in the other.

In 1913, totally unexpectedly, he received notice that his last surviving brother had died childless and that he was now Lord Ashburnham. His wife "the Telephone Girl" became the mistress of a vast estate which included a hundred-room mansion. Her stay in England was not that enjoyable since she was not accepted by the Ashburnham family. As a result Lord and Lady Ashburnham moved back to Fredericton in 1914 and became the centre of "an elite social life in the Fredericton community." Lord Ashburnham continued to spend part of the year in Fredericton and part of the year in England until he died in 1924 while on a visit to England. His wife continued to occupy the house until her death in reduced circumstances in 1938. Since that time the building has had numerous owners and fallen into decay, but Lady Ashburnham's name is still fresh in the minds of many in the Fredericton area because of her favourite pickle recipe.

ASHBURNHAM HOUSE

Carman House, "Cosey Cottage"
(83 Shore Street)

During his lifetime, Bliss Carman was a poet of the first rank in both the United States and Canada. He published his first book of poems, *Low Tide at Grand Pré*, in 1893 and his best-known book is *Songs from Vagabondia*, written with Richard Hovey. He was the cousin of another well-known Fredericton writer, Sir Charles G.D. Roberts. For many years, this building, which was called Cosey Cottage, was Bliss Carman's home.

The middle part of the house was built by Col. George Shore around 1840 for his daughter and son-in-law, Richard Pennyfeather, who was secretary to Lieutenant-Governor Sir Edmund Head. It was built to front on a road which Col. Shore had staked out, but this road was never constructed; as a result, the front of the house, with its many French doors, faces the garden and its large elm trees. The footpath at the back of the house became "Gas Alley" after the gas works was built at its University Avenue end, and the path was later named Shore Street. After Col. Shore's death in 1851, the house was sold to Henry Robinson, who purchased land to the west of the house and added a new wing. A second gable was added to the house in 1860. The poet's father, William Carman, purchased the house around 1867, and Bliss, who was born in 1861, lived there until young manhood. From his bedroom window he could see the beautiful Saint John River, where he spent a lot of time in his canoe.

Carman's parents were both dead by 1886, and for a time his sister Muriel and their aunt ran Cosey Cottage as a boarding house for university students. Carman was living in the United States by 1890, and in that year he sold his share in the cottage to his sister. Sometime after this, the cottage was sold to a cousin, Frederick St. John Bliss. In 1965 his daughters sold it to Col. G. D. Dailley, who renovated it extensively.

Ferrando Pupils /97

CARMAN HOUSE

The Old Rectory

(734 George Street)

This square brick house is one of Fredericton's famous literary homes. It was first occupied by the Rev. George Coster, who was appointed Archdeacon of New Brunswick and Rector of Fredericton in October 1829. In 1831, the year after the Costers arrived in Fredericton, they lost most of their possessions in two house fires within five months. As a result, the vestry decided to build the rector a proper house of brick or stone. The Hon. W.F. Odell, who was Provincial Secretary at the time, provided two lots on George Street as a site for the new rectory. Constructed in the Georgian style and made of bricks imported from England, its two and a half storeys were capped by a slate roof. It was completed in 1833.

The Costers used this attractive and spacious house thoroughly. Prominent in Fredericton society, they were noted for their enjoyable parties, with popular and sacred music and discussions and readings from Shakespeare, Dickens and Thackeray. The Coster daughters all married advantageously in the community.

After George Coster's death in 1859, the Rev. Charles Lee moved into the rectory, followed in 1873 by the Rev. Canon George Goodridge Roberts, "a scholarly gentleman of old English descent," who was rector of Christ Church Parish Church (St. Anne's) for thirty-two years. His children figure prominently in Canada's literary history. The most famous was the eldest, Charles G.D. Roberts, who wrote a number of books of poetry including *Orion and Other Poems* and *The Vagrant of Time*. Often called "the Father of Canadian literature," Charles is best known for his collections of stories such as *The Kindred of the Wild* and *The Backwoodsmen*. Canon Roberts's other two sons, Theodore Goodridge Roberts and William Carman Roberts, were also well-known literary figures, and his daughter, Jane Elizabeth Gostwick Roberts MacDonald, had her share of literary fame as well.

The Old Rectory was surrounded on three sides by beautiful lawns and elm-shaded gardens. The Roberts teenagers and their cousin Bliss Carman used to congregate there, and Mrs. C.F. Fraser wrote an idyllic Victorian picture of them:

> *In summer weather the great old-fashioned garden, haunt of all fragrant and time-honoured flowers, was the favourite spot. There, in and about the hammocks, with their cousin, Bliss Carman, extending his great length on the grass below, and shaggy Nestor, wisest of all household dogs, wandering about from one to another, with half-tamed birds fluttering and twittering in the trees above, these young people did indeed see visions and dream dreams.*

The Old Rectory was sold to Walter Limerick in 1914; it has been owned by the Limerick family ever since, and except for its shingled roof, it has not been altered significantly.

THE OLD RECTORY

Little Glencoe
(745 George Street)

Across the street from the Church of England Rectory on George Street, a much more modest wooden house with "Halifax or Scottish gables" was built in 1847 by the Rev. Daniel McCurdy, a Presbyterian minister. This house, "Little Glencoe," was sold in 1850 to Mary Grosvenor, the wife of a prominent Fredericton merchant. It was occupied for many years by two daughters of Capt. William Bailey of the Loyal American Regiment, Miss Elizabeth Bailey and Mrs. Ann Emerson, the widow of the former surgeon to the 104th Regiment. Miss Bailey lived to be one hundred and six,

Little Glencoe

and at her funeral the ladies of Fredericton marched in the funeral procession to the old Loyalist graveyard, where both sisters are buried. In 1872 the house was purchased by Dr. George Roberts, the father of Canon George Goodridge Roberts and the retired headmaster of the Fredericton Collegiate School. His granddaughter, Jane Elizabeth Gostwick Roberts MacDonald, and her husband lived in Little Glencoe after their marriage in 1896. She wrote poems, stories and essays, and, with her brothers William Carman Roberts and Theodore Goodridge Roberts, published *Northland Lyrics* in 1899. In 1906 she published *Dream Verses and Others*. The small east wing of the house had one room which she called the Library, and it was there that she did her writing. She encouraged her son, Cuthbert Goodridge MacDonald, and his friends to write when they were young children, and Cuthbert, too, became a poet and journalist.

Three George Street Houses

(759, 769 and 777)

THREE GEORGE STREET HOUSES

There are many attractive houses on George Street, and the three in this painting reflect different architectural styles of the nineteenth century. The oldest of the three, on the left, was built in 1826 by Alward Harned, a mason and carpenter who worked on the construction of Government House. In 1860, his son-law, James White, a watchmaker, lived there. White built a large telescope in the garden, and neighbours and friends visited frequently to scan the skies. Over the years the front of the house was rebuilt, the door was replaced, and an end porch was added.

The yellow house next door was built between 1878 and 1882. The original owner was Henry Clark, a carpenter who lived in the third of these houses. The house has interesting trim and latticed ornaments, and Clark may have built it himself. The story goes that Mr. Clark, the owner of what was then a vacant lot, built the house to separate himself from his neighbour, with whom he did not get along.

The third house in the painting was built on a lot purchased by George Segee in 1855. The house was built in 1860 by Harry A. Clark, and his son, Henry B. Clark, may have expanded it in the 1870s when he lived here.

Somerville House

(238 Waterloo Row)

In 1974 this most impressive home became the residence of the lieutenant-governor. It was built or rebuilt in 1866, after a fire had all but destroyed the original house on this site, which had been constructed in 1816 for Judge John Murray Bliss. That house had been purchased in 1845 by the Hon. Charles Fisher, a Father of Confederation, who named it Somerville House after Dr. James Somerville, the first president of King's College (now the University of New Brunswick), whom he had admired when he was a student there. Fisher had also defended the college in the legislature when some members attempted to have it closed down. Around 1866 the building was partially destroyed by fire. Some of the mahogany doors and windows and other material was saved, and what was left of the building was redesigned and renovated. Fisher had a large, fashionable garden party when the work was finished.

After Fisher's death in 1881, his daughter changed the name of the house to Summer Villa. It was later bequeathed to the University of New Brunswick by Fisher's last surviving daughter. The university, not having any use for it at the time and being in need of money, sold it at auction in 1909 to Charles H. Thomas, a merchant who became mayor of Fredericton. After his death, the house was occupied by a number of tenants including Brigadier General Frederick William Hill and his daughter, Louise Hill, a well-known local historian.

In 1948 Lord Beaverbrook took a fancy to the house and purchased it. It was thought at the time that he would establish a home here, but after extensive renovations were completed he gave it to the University of New Brunswick as a residence for the president. From 1959 to 1968 it housed the Law School, which had been moved from Saint John. When the new law school opened on campus, Somerville House was rented to the provincial government and used for offices until 1973. Then the government bought the building and converted it into a residence for the lieutenant-governor. When renovations to Government House on Woodstock Road, now underway, are completed and it once more becomes the residence of the lieutenant-governor, Somerville House will again need new tenants.

SOMERVILLE HOUSE

Harrison House

(92 Waterloo Row)

There was a building on this lot at the corner of Shore Street and Waterloo Row which Andrew Mareau, a blacksmith, leased from Col. George Shore in 1819. It was occupied by a number of people over the years, and it is uncertain whether the original building was altered over the years or whether it was replaced by a new structure before it was purchased in 1874 by Dr. Thomas Harrison, who had been appointed Professor of English literature at the University of New Brunswick in 1870. Harrison, a native of Sheffield, New Brunswick, may have been

HARRISON HOUSE

COURTESY OF THE CITY OF FREDERICTON

responsible for the very attractive "Maugerville trim" which is the most interesting feature of this house. Dr. Harrison and his wife lived here until he was appointed president of the University of New Brunswick in 1885. A number of people owned the house at various times after that until it passed into the hands of the Hon. John B. McNair, who was premier of the province for twelve years, chief justice for ten years and lieutenant-governor from 1965 until his death in 1968. It is now owned by his son, the Hon. John C. McNair.

NEIL FARM

(295 Neil Street)

The Neil farm, the only operating farm within today's city limits, was established by John Neil, a Scot. Neil arrived in New Brunswick in 1839 and opened a hardware business in Fredericton. In 1856 he purchased a lot containing two hundred acres, "more or less," fronting on the Saint John River in St. Marys, where he established a farm. It has been operated by the Neil family for four generations. The original farm house was located at the bottom of the hill near the river. The present house, which sits high on a hill overlooking Devon, was built sometime after

NEIL FARM

1878. At present the farm consists of 235 acres plus 100 rented acres. It is worked by Albert and Ron Neil and one helper, and they have a herd of 115 Holsteins. As the city expands their farm becomes more and more valuable to developers, and it may soon disappear, since it is now too valuable to sell as farmland. It has been suggested that the city should buy the farm to develop a green space for the north side of the river comparable to Odell Park on the south side. The brothers are reluctant to sell their farm, but because there are no Neils left who are interested in farming, its days are numbered.

Hatt House

(292 Canada Street)

This house is located on a stretch of Canada Street that was sometimes referred to as "Nob Hill" because it was home to the Gibsons and their mill managers, the elite of Marysville. The Hatt House is the largest and most handsome of the houses built by Alexander (Boss) Gibson for cotton mill officials. It is two and a half storeys high, with scalloped shingles on the gable ends of the attic and a double-door entrance with stained glass windows. On the second storey there is another stained glass window with a small decorative wooden fan above. It was built in 1885 for Charles Hatt, Gibson's principal bookkeeper, future mill manager, and son-in-law. He had married Annie Gibson in 1883, and their wedding was as elaborate a celebration as Boss Gibson could make it, with a brass band, fireworks and a gala reception to which everyone who showed up for the outside festivities was invited. Hatt was a member of Marysville's first town council, and he later served a term as mayor.

HATT HOUSE

Neville Homestead
(UNB Campus)

The Neville homestead was built in 1878, and the farm originally adjoined land owned by the university. For many years the Neville family supplied labour, firewood and produce to the University of New Brunswick. In the 1950s the university needed more land for residences and wanted to buy the farm from Fred Neville. Fred had started working for the university in 1912, looking after the grounds and cutting grass and firewood, and he had continued to do so for thirty-five years. Fred agreed to sell the farm on condition that he be allowed to live in the homestead until his death. This was agreeable to President Colin B. McKay, but he wanted the house moved, since it was sitting right where a new residence was supposed to go. In exchange for moving the building, Dr. McKay promised to name the new residence Neville House. Mr. Neville agreed to this, and the homestead was moved down the hill a short distance to its present location. He continued to live there until he died in 1969 at the age of 91. The building now houses the university's public relations department and information office.

NEVILLE HOMESTEAD

COURTESY OF VERA ZAROWSKY

The Maggie Jean Chestnut Residence

(511 Charlotte Street)

This Victorian house on the corner of Charlotte and Church streets was built in the late 1890s on land purchased in April 1894 by Mary Ann Fraser from Charles Odell. Frederick St. John Bliss bought the house in May 1900 and, three months later, sold it to the Bank of Montreal. It was used as a residence for the bank's managers until it was sold to Lord Beaverbrook in 1948. This led, in 1949, to the realization of the long-time dream of the University of New Brunswick Alumnae Society to provide a residence for female students, when Lord Beaverbrook agreed to give it to them on condition that they raise enough money to renovate and equip it by 31 December 1949. They were successful, and the residence was opened with a coffee party in October 1949 attended by Lord Beaverbrook and Mrs. H.G. Chestnut, who became the first president of the Alumnae Society in 1911. The building was named after her daughter, Maggie Jean, an active member of the alumnae, who had died in February 1949.

THE MAGGIE JEAN CHESTNUT RESIDENCE

Jewett House
(777 King Street)

The Jewett house was built in 1897 for A.J. Edgecombe, a prominent businessman who owned Edgecombe's Carriage Factory on the corner of King and York streets. Located just around the corner from Bishopscote and the Crockett House, this building is said to be one of the best examples of Queen Anne Revival architecture in Fredericton. Its most noteworthy features are its corner tower and its dormer windows of various sizes. It also has a distinctive bay window, front entrance and tall decorative chimney. Before this house could be built, the MacAdam House (779 King Street), which was constructed in 1845, had to be moved from its original site on the corner of Secretary Lane. This new and much more elaborate mansion was owned for many years by Dr. B.L. Jewett. It was sold to the province in the 1960s and is now government offices.

JEWETT HOUSE

Bishopscote and Dunrobin or Crockett House

(97 Church Street & 796 Queen Street)

Bishopscote was built in 1848-1849 by Benjamin Wolhaupter, a watchmaker, a successful businessman, a director of both the Commer cial Bank of New Brunswick and the St. Andrews and Quebec Railway, and the Commissioner of Public Buildings. In 1847 he was appointed High Sheriff of York County, and he was involved in assisting sick emigrants who arrived in Fredericton as a result of the Great Irish Famine. He was very active in church affairs and a friend and admirer of Bishop John Medley. Wolhaupter died in 1857, and in 1866 Bishop Medley purchased his former home, which from then on was called Bishopscote. According to Juliana Horatia Ewing, the bishop left this house every day for morning service at seven-thirty, walking into the cathedral "with a pastoral staff much bigger than himself." Some people claim to see the ghost of Mrs. Margaret Medley leaving Bishopscote on her way to the cathedral, which she enters by the west door, and some also say she is accompanied by a small dog. Bishop Medley died in 1892, and Margaret Medley continued to occupy the house until her death in 1905. The next owner, William Turney Whitehead, a land agent and former mayor of Fredericton, enlarged and altered the appearance of the house considerably, adding a turret, stained glass windows and verandas and changing its name to Beauregard. It is now owned by Mr. and Mrs. Ronald Miller.

The building on the corner of Queen and Church streets, next door to Bishopscote, was constructed around the turn of the century by George Dibblee. An old log cabin or cottage had stood on this lot for over one hundred years, since before the original town plat was laid out. The lot had been purchased in 1789 by Peter Fraser and his partner, James Brannen. When they divided the lot, Brannen retained the corner portion and the old house, while Fraser constructed Cambourne House, now Farraline Place, on the upper part. Dibblee tore down the old house and built a new one, which he called Dunrobin. It eventually became the home of Dr. and Mrs. Pierce Crockett. In 1963 Dunrobin was purchased by the provincial government, and for many years it housed government offices, including the department of tourism. It now houses Gallery 78, a commercial art gallery.

If there is a ghost that visits the cathedral from the vicinity of Bishopscote and Dunrobin, perhaps it isn't Mrs. Medley. Perhaps it is Miss Fanny Berton, the sister-in-law of Peter Fraser, who lived in the log cabin until her death in 1873, aged 93. Juliana Horatia Ewing describes Fanny Berton in *Mrs. Overtheway's Remembrances*:

The little old lady lived over the way through a green gate that shut with a click, and up three white steps. Every morning at eight o'clock the church bells chimed for morning prayer — chime! chime! chime!chime! — and every morning at eight o'clock the little old lady came down the white steps and opened the gate with a click, and went where the bells were calling.

BISHOPSCOTE AND DUNROBIN OR CROCKETT HOUSE

The University of New Brunswick President's House

(58 Waterloo Row)

This house was built in 1910 for Arthur Gibson, the son of Boss Gibson and a prominent Fredericton merchant, on part of a three-and-a-half-acre lot. This lot once contained three houses which were purchased for Gen. Benedict Arnold in 1786. One of the buildings was the Golden Ball Inn, where Juliana Horatia Ewing, an English author of children's stories, lived while her husband was attached to the Fredericton garrison in the 1860s. In her stories she called this building Reka Dom. Arthur Gibson built his new mansion just upriver from the site of the old inn, which was demolished in 1909. Like a number of late nineteenth and early twentieth-century buildings in the downtown area and along Waterloo Row, the house was built in the Classical Revival style, with ionic capitals surmounting pillars in a configuration which is sometimes referred to as Classical Plantation. Over the years a number of prominent politicians and government figures lived in this house, including Lieutenant Governor Murray McLaren, Chief Justice J.E. Michaud and Premier Louis J. Robichaud, who sold the house to the University of New Brunswick in 1973. Since that time it has been the home of the university's president.

The University of New Brunswick President's House

PUBLIC BUILDINGS

All Saints Anglican Church

(172 Canada Street, Marysville)

In 1892, the Rev. John Parkinson, rector of St. Mary's, had architects prepare plans for the construction of the first Anglican church in Marysville. In the same year land was purchased near the site of the old lumber mill by the Nashwaak River, and a mission hall was built there. Before construction of the church began, Alexander (Boss) Gibson gave St. Mary's parish land which was thought to be a better site for a church. Construction began in 1893, and the mission hall was used as a church until the new building was completed; raising the necessary funds took time, and it was not finished until 1899. It was renovated and expanded in the 1960s.

All Saints Anglican Church

St. Anthony's Roman Catholic Church

(603 Union Street, Devon)

When the new Roman Catholic parish of St. Anthony was formed in 1887, there was no church in St. Marys and the majority of Catholics in the area lived on the St. Mary's Reserve. The first rector, Father John Keirnan, celebrated mass in the schoolhouse there while a small church was being constructed. As the congregation grew, this little church was enlarged, but by 1890, it was once again too small. In 1901, Father J.J. Ryan, who took over the parish in 1895, began the construction of a much larger and more beautiful church. The old church was moved to the back of the lot and was used as a church hall until it was demolished in the 1950s. The new wood-framed church was built in the Gothic style, with two small twelve-foot-square towers and a taller ninety one foot tower with a belfry; this was torn down in the 1960s and replaced with a shorter one. The stone for the foundation came from the demolished Hermitage, which was owned by St. Dunstan's parish. St. Anthony's, completed in 1906, is now the oldest Roman Catholic church in Fredericton.

Fernando Poyatos/97

St. Anthony's Roman Catholic Church

St. Anne's Chapel of Ease (Christ Church Parish Church)

(245 Westmorland Street)

St. Anne's Chapel of Ease is one of the best English Gothic Revival small parish churches in North America. Bishop John Medley, who introduced this style to the continent, had the chapel constructed to show New Brunswickers what a neo-Gothic church should look like: it was modelled on ancient chapels in existence in England in Henry III's day. The land was provided by the Hon. John Saunders, and Saunders, Bishop Medley, and the architect, Frank Wills, laid the cornerstone on 5 June 1846. The walls were made of stone and the roof of butternut, open on the inside and covered on the outside with slate. A stone archway with a butternut screen separates the nave and chancel. St. Anne's even has a medieval-style lych gate, a wooden structure with a roof and open sides built at the entrance to the churchyard to protect the coffin and the pall bearers from bad weather while they awaited the funeral procession or the clergyman. Although held up to New Brunswick Anglicans as an example of the best style of church building, St. Anne's offended some who saw it as evidence of Bishop Medley's desire to introduce "popish rites and ceremonies." Its stained glass windows, textured designs on the chancel wall, ornamented floor tiles and wood carvings were taken as proof of Medley's "dark and most insidious design," as was his insistence that all pews be open and free, rather than rented as was the custom.

On completion, St. Anne's Chapel of Ease could hold a hundred and seventy-five people. By 1956 the congregation had increased to over four hundred, and a new parish church was needed. Construction began in 1960, using a steel frame, stone from a local quarry, limestone from Indiana, redwood from California and tile from Italy. Everything was done to make the new building a suitable addition to the Gothic Revival chapel. The organ was moved to the new church, and a passageway connects the two. In this way, the heritage building is preserved and used on suitable occasions, while the modern building serves the daily needs of a large and active congregation.

St. Anne's Chapel of Ease (Christ Church Parish Church)

CHRIST CHURCH CATHEDRAL

(Corner of Brunswick and Church Streets)

Christ Church Cathedral is an architectural gem in an ideal setting. It was the first entirely new cathedral built on British soil between the Norman Conquest and 1853, and the first Anglican cathedral to be built after the Reformation. It is also one of the earliest and best examples of the nineteenth-century revival of decorated Gothic architecture in North America. It fulfilled the dream of Bishop John Medley, New Brunswick's first Church of England bishop, who raised the funds for its construction. When he died in 1892 he was buried outside the east end of the cathedral, and his effigy lies at the southeast corner of the nave.

When it was known that Bishop Medley intended to build a cathedral, many people in Saint John felt that it should be built there and not in Fredericton. "Observer," writing in a Saint John newspaper, claimed: "The ground is a perfect mire and I should not be surprised to see the whole concern sink — that is, if it ever floats at all." A week later, the same writer commented that the bishop was going ahead with his plans, "provided the Fredericton folk will subscribe *FIVE THOUSAND POUNDS* toward it. That they will never do!" The bishop was not worried. Within weeks of his having made his intentions known he had commitments totalling four thousand pounds, and he received large sums from supporters in Britain and the United States, always at opportune times when funds were running low.

The cathedral was designed by Frank Wills, an architect brought by Medley from England, who also designed some fifty churches in the United States. The cornerstone was laid on 15 October 1845, and the cathedral was consecrated on 31 August 1853. The stone used in the construction of the building came from Grindstone Island in Shepody Bay, and dressed stone for the windows and doorways came from Caen, in Normandy.

In July 1911 the cathedral spire was struck by lightning and collapsed in the resulting fire. The eight bells, which weighed almost five tons, all melted, the roof was badly damaged, and many windows were broken. Under the direction of J. DeLancy Robinson, a local architect, the spire was rebuilt twenty-eight feet higher than before, which was what the original plans had called for. A shorter spire had been necessary at the time of construction because of a shortage of funds. The new spire was given a chime of fifteen bells by Sir James Dunn, a native of Bathurst, New Brunswick.

CHRIST CHURCH CATHEDRAL

Bishop's Court

(791 Brunswick Street)

Very close to the Cathedral, on the corner of Brunswick and Church streets, is a Victorian-style home built around the turn of the century with a hip roof and dormer windows. Since 1943, it has been the residence of the Anglican Bishop of New Brunswick and is referred to as Bishop's Court.

BISHOP'S COURT

Diocesan Synod of Fredericton

(115 Church Street)

This large Victorian house, built around 1870, is shown on a map of 1878. At that time it was owned by D.F. George, a merchant. It now contains the offices of the Diocesan Synod of Fredericton. It is next door to Bishop's Court.

DIOCESAN SYNOD OF FREDERICTON

Wilmot United Church
(473 King Street)

The origins of Wilmot United Church can be traced back to 1791, when thirteen Fredericton Methodists, led by Duncan Blair, met to form a Methodist Society. For almost twenty years they had no place of worship, but in 1810 they built a small chapel on the north side of King Street near Northumberland Street. By 1830 their numbers had grown; they purchased land on the corner of King and Carleton streets, and in January 1832 they consecrated their new five-hundred-seat chapel. By 1839 this chapel was also too small, so they added a twenty-foot extension and a steeple. On 1 November 1850 the church was destroyed in the worst fire in Fredericton's history, which left few buildings standing between Carleton and St. John streets.

Plans were made immediately to build an even bigger church, and Matthew Stead, a well know architect from Saint John, was hired to design it. The result was a magnificent wooden Gothic church which was dedicated in December 1852. Wilmot Methodist could seat over twelve hundred people; for more than a century it was the largest auditorium in the city. The 194-foot steeple was surmounted by a twelve-and-a-half-foot hand with the index finger pointing to heaven, which made the church the tallest building in Fredericton. British soldiers stationed at the military compound called it "Thumbs Up."

By 1970 there was concern that the unique hand on the steeple might fall over. An inspection by a steeplejack showed deep rot in the tower; "Thumbs Up" was twenty-five feet off the vertical. The cost of repairs was prohibitive, so the hand had to come down and the height of the steeple was reduced. The hand can now be seen in a glass case in the church hall.

WILMOT UNITED CHURCH

Brunswick Street United Baptist Church

(161 Brunswick Street)

Baptists were active in the Fredericton area as early as 1792, and in 1814 their first church, the Free Will Baptist Church, was established by the Rev. Elijah Estabrooks on the north side of King Street down-river from Regent Street.

The church started with thirteen members, but numbers grew, and in 1836 a Baptist seminary was opened on York Street between George and Brunswick. Two years later, in 1838, plans were drawn up for a new wooden church, which was constructed nearby on the corner of Brunswick and York. It was extensively repaired in 1881, only to be destroyed by a fire in 1882.

The cornerstone for the present church was laid in the same year, and a fine stone building with Gothic features was opened in November 1883. The interior followed Baptist tradition, with a central pulpit surrounded by semi-circular seating, balconies and Gothic decorations. Like St. Paul's United Church, which was constructed a few years later, the steeple was attached to the side instead of being supported by the main structure, a departure from Gothic tradition. The arches were shortened in the construction of the main body of the church to allow for a lower ceiling than usual in churches built in the Gothic style. Among the many changes made to the church in this century are the addition of a pipe organ and the construction of a new wing to provide space for a gym and Sunday school classrooms.

BRUNSWICK STREET BAPTIST CHURCH

St. Paul's United Church

(224 York Street)

St. Paul's United Church was constructed in 1886 on the site of the Auld Kirk, a Presbyterian church built in 1832 by Mr. Fitzpatrick from plans drawn up by William Taylor, who had donated the land in 1828. The old church was designed as a "preaching box" along the lines of the meeting houses and congregational churches built in New Brunswick at that time; it seated about six hundred. In 1843 some members broke away from the church to form a Free Kirk, and they remained separated until 1874. In 1881, the reunited and rapidly growing congregation decided that a larger church was needed to accommodate the 1127 members. Before construction began, the Auld Kirk was moved to the rear of the lot and turned to face York Street. It became the Sunday school after the new church was opened in 1886.

Like Brunswick St. Baptist Church, the new St. Paul's is an excellent example of the post-Medley-style New Brunswick church which was not an exact Gothic reproduction. The Gothic form was used for decorative purposes, but changes were made in the architecture — such as the positioning of the tower — for reasons of style. In 1916, a new church hall, Fraser Memorial Hall, was opened, the Old Kirk having been moved once more and converted into the Kirk Apartments at 433 Charlotte Street. In 1925, after church union, St. Paul's Presbyterian became St. Paul's United Church, but some dissenters left the congregation and formed St. Andrew's Presbyterian Church on Charlotte Street.

St. Paul's Church

COURTESY OF JOANNE AND REID MANORE

Holy Trinity Church

(Lower St. Marys)

Holy Trinity Church, Lower St. Marys, stands on the top of the hill just above the Peppers House. Built on land donated by Col. Peppers and George Sterling, it faces the Saint John River, since at the time of its construction the road was expected to run along the river bank. Holy Trinity was finished in 1846 and consecrated by Bishop John Medley in 1848. It was erected over two unidentified graves, and other unmarked graves were scattered over the hillside. Many of the early Loyalists who settled in the Lower St. Marys area and worshipped at Holy Trinity are buried in the churchyard.

Designed to hold eighty people, Holy Trinity is one of the earliest and most interesting of the neo-Gothic churches on which Frank Wills, the English architect, and Bishop John Medley collaborated. Because it was built in the form of a cross, it is often called the Little Cross Church. Each arm of the cross is of equal length. Parishioners would sit in two of the arms, the choir and vestry would sit in the third, and the chancel occupies the east arm. This design was very unusual, and Bishop Medley claimed, "Cross Churches are very pleasing in effect when small, and the arms nearly equal, but cannot be recommended in large Churches." The church has many features of the Gothic revival, with triple-lancet windows at the ends of the north, west and east arms, smaller double-lancet windows at the end of the south arm, and single lancet windows in the side walls. It is topped by an elegant open belfry over the centre of the cross. Construction was supervised by William Jaffrey, who served as rector from 1851 to 1890.

After the construction of St. Mary's in Devon in 1873, Holy Trinity faced demolition on several occasions. Early this century the church was closed. A newspaper in the 1930s reported that the old church, which had been closed for ten years or more because of a lack of worshippers, had been recently repaired and was again open. The old bell, which had been removed to the parish church in Devon, had "pealed forth again," and the church was filled to the doors. The church was again deserted between 1933 and 1945. In the 1980s it once again faced demolition but was saved by volunteers who began restoration in 1987. The work still continues, and the church, designated a Provincial Historic Site, remains closed for regular services.

Holy Trinity Church

The Hartt Shoe Factory

(401 York Street)

Constructed in 1898, this three-storey brick building, which is fifty feet wide and two hundred feet long, is the oldest surviving shoe factory in the Atlantic Provinces. The building was designed to look like the Marysville Cotton Mill and other factories established in the Maritime Provinces and New England during the late nineteenth century. It was constructed for ten businessmen who formed the Hartt Boot and Shoe Company in 1898. By 1913 between two hundred and two hundred and fifty employees produced between eight hundred and a thousand pairs of shoes daily. They were shipped by the boxcar load to Winnipeg, Calgary, and Vancouver for further distribution everywhere in Canada, and they sold for five to ten dollars a pair. The company was said to be the only shoe factory in Canada that manufactured "men's high grade shoes only," and this, plus the good sense of the owners, was the secret of the company's success.

Over time, Hartt's specialty shoes came to include golf shoes, curling shoes, shoes for railway men, and boots for the Royal Canadian Mounted Police, the police of five American states, the Newfoundland Rangers and the British Columbia Provincial Police. In 1949, the company boasted that its shoes had been worn by King George VI, the Duke of Windsor, and two prime ministers of Canada, as well as Buster Lightfinger, a famous circus midget, and by the constable with the largest feet in the RCMP. In the early 1930s, their golf shoes had caught the eye of the Duke of York, who became George VI, and his brother, the Duke of Windsor, briefly King Edward VIII. They and other elite golfers considered Hartt shoes more fashionable than similar shoes produced in the United States. The two prime ministers who wore Hartt shoes were R.B. Bennett, a Conservative, and William Lyon Mackenzie King, a Liberal.

By 1949, mechanization had reduced the number of Hartt employees to a hundred and fifty, but they still shipped shoes all over Canada as well as to South Africa, New Zealand, Australia, Great Britain, the United States, Bermuda, Jamaica and Trinidad. In 1998 the company is still the only manufacturer of the high boots worn by the RCMP and various police forces in Canada and the United States.

HARTT SHOE FACTORY

Marysville Cotton Mill

(20 McGloin Street, Marysville)

The Marysville Cotton Mill was constructed by Alexander (Boss) Gibson, who operated lumber mills in the area. For years he had been driving forty million feet of logs down the Nashwaak River annually to his mills. He had also built twenty-four low wooden double-tenement houses on River Street for his workers. Some of these stand today, some were removed when the cotton mill was built, and others burned and were rebuilt. Gibson wanted his new cotton mill to be larger than the one at Milltown in Charlotte County, which at that time was the largest cotton mill in Canada. In 1882 he brought in an architect from New England to plan the construction, and he started his own brickyard, since he wanted the bricks to be produced locally. The cornerstone was laid in May 1883, and the roof was completed on New Years Day 1884. Given the size of the main building — which is four storeys high, four hundred and eighteen feet long and a hundred feet wide — the speed of its construction amazed everyone. A wing was later added which was a hundred and ninety-eight feet long and ninety-eight feet wide. The mill was very modern in its internal design: it was heated by steam, it had a sprinkler system through-out in case of fire, and it was illuminated by eight hundred electric lights.

MARYSVILLE COTTON MILL

Marysville Cotton Mill Workers' Homes

(Morrison Street)

Since no one in Marysville knew how to do the highly skilled work of manufacturing cotton, Gibson had to import workers from England and the United States. To house them he built fifty-eight brick houses, as well as a brick store and a brick hotel. Originally the mill had between two hundred and three hundred employees, who were paid during their on-the-job-training. There were good schools in the area; a six-room company house with running water could be rented for four dollars per month; and an eight room house cost eight dollars. Conditions were so good that Gibson never had trouble keeping his employees, and Canadian Cotton continued his paternalistic policies after they took over in 1911. They modernized the factory, which increased production to the point that, in 1913, the mill had an output of fifty to eighty thousand pounds of finished cotton a week. It had sixteen thousand spindles and a thousand looms in operation, and between seven hundred and eight hundred employees. Two eight-hundred-horse-power coal-fired compound engines provided power for the operation. In 1913, Canadian Cotton announced their determination to make Marysville "the model mill town of America." They built more houses to accommodate new workers, and they claimed that the workers earned such good wages that no one left except "through marriage or families moving away." By 1949 the mill still had six hundred and fifty employees and

operated from seven in the morning to midnight with two shifts. In 1954 the company fell into financial difficulties and closed the mill. It was opened again in 1957 and struggled along under a number of owners until it finally shut down in the 1970s. The bell tower was removed at that time, and the provincial government took possession of the mill and renovated it for government offices. Today the mill building and the surviving workers' homes provide one of the best examples of a nineteenth-century mill town to be found anywhere in eastern North America.

Marysville Cotton Mill Worker's Homes

King's College

(The Old Arts Building, University of New Brunswick)

In 1824 the House of Assembly was persuaded to provide funds for the construction of a college to replace the College of New Brunswick. A spacious building was to be constructed "of rough stone of the Country," not more than two storeys high, with rooms for a president, vice-president, one or two professors, twenty students, and servants. It was also to contain a chapel, a dining room, classrooms and a library — in all, a total of forty-two rooms. King's College was designed by J.E. Woolford, who also designed Government House, and the foundation stone was laid in 1825 by Lieutenant-Governor Sir Howard Douglas, the first chancellor of King's College. It was opened on 1 January 1829. Now called the Old Arts Building, it is the oldest university building in Canada still in use.

Originally King's College was two storeys high, and in the early years all students lived there, guaranteed "good and sufficient board and beer." For almost a hundred years all college life took place within the walls of King's College or on the surrounding lawns. In the early years students were not encouraged to go to town, permission was needed to visit an inn, a tavern "or a place of amusement," and there was a ten o'clock curfew. Among the most famous students were Bliss Carman, Sir Charles G.D. Roberts and Sir George Foster, at one time Canada's representative to the League of Nations.

One famous teacher was Douglas Hyde, a Gaelic scholar who became the first president of the Irish Republic. One of the more infamous residents, a college official who had been indulging too liberally, rode his horse up the front steps and into the Great Hall, where he discharged his pistols into the ceiling.

The Old Arts Building has two magnificent stained glass windows which are memorials to Col. Thomas Carleton, the province's first governor, and Sir Howard Douglas. In 1878 the building was renovated and a third storey with a mansard roof was added to provide space for a library and a laboratory. In 1963 the chapel, which still has the original benches and desktops extensively carved with student's initials and graffiti, was extensively renovated. The building has been designated a National Historic Site.

KING'S COLLEGE

Brydone Jack Observatory and McCord Hall

The Observatory, built in 1851, was the first in Canada. University of New Brunswick president William Brydone Jack used it to determine the longitude of Fredericton and to correct errors in the international border between New Brunswick and Maine. It has served as an art centre, faculty club, and headquarters for *The Fiddlehead*. It is now a museum.

The small building next to it is McCord Hall, which was built around 1851 as the university ice house. Originally scheduled for demolition, it was moved to its current location in 1959. Partially rebuilt and furnished, it became a senior study room and later a centre where writers such as Nancy and Bill Bauer, Kent Thompson, Ted Colson and Robert Gibbs — labelled by Alden Nowlan "The Icehouse Gang" — could meet.

BRYDONE JACK OBSERVATORY AND MCCORD HALL

COURTESY OF COLIN B. MACKAY

Memorial Hall

Memorial Hall, which was used for over thirty Encaenias, was built as a memorial to thirty-five University of New Brunswick alumni who died during World War I. Attempts to raise funds for this purpose began in 1914 and continued until finally, in 1923, the first major step in the construction of the building was taken: Lord Byng, the Governor General and a commander of the Canadian Forces during World War I, laid the cornerstone. The building has seven stained glass windows, two of which were installed in 1926. One was presented by Lady Ashburnham in memory of her husband, and the second is a memorial to George Fenwick (Class of 1902), who died at Passchendaele. The auditorium remains in constant use, and the building also houses the university Art Centre and the resident musicians.

MEMORIAL HALL

COURTESY OF GISÈLE LEBLANC AND ROBERT SKILLEN

Forestry-Geology Building
and Bonar Law-Bennett Library

The Forestry-Geology Building (left), which took two years to complete, was opened in 1931 after funding was provided by the province on the understanding that the Department of Lands and Mines could be housed there. Originally it was also supposed to contain a new library, but instead the government presented the university with a separate building (right) which had the capacity to house 100,000 volumes.

Lord Beaverbrook added a new wing to this library in 1951 and donated 50,000 books, including the 12,000-volume Beaverbrook Collection, as well as the collected papers of Andrew Bonar Law, the only Canadian to become Prime Minister of England, and the papers of R.B. Bennett, a former prime minister of Canada, both of whom were born in New Brunswick. It was at this time that the building was named the Bonar Law-Bennett Library. When the Harriet Irving Library opened in 1966, the Bonar Law-Bennett Library became the home of the Provincial Archives of New Brunswick.

FORESTRY-GEOLOGY BUILDING AND BONAR LAW–BENNETT LIBRARY

LADY BEAVERBROOK RESIDENCE

The University of New Brunswick's first residence,
the Lady Beaverbrook Residence, was the gift of Lord
Beaverbrook in 1935 in memory of his first wife.
Equipped with a swimming pool, squash courts, a dining
hall with a minstrels' gallery, panelled lounges, and rooms
for a hundred and twenty students, it looked — and to
some extent functioned — like a gentleman's club.
In the 1950s and 1960s female students were admitted
to the residence for summer school, when women lived
on one side of the building and men on the other. Since
1985 it has been coeducational year-round. A distinguish-
ing feature of the building is its impressive clock tower,
with a beaver weather vane and quarter-hour chimes which
play one of Lord Beaverbrook's favourite Miramichi folk
songs, "The Jones Boys." The clock is only partially
functional now, and the chimes play only on special
occasions.

Lady Beaverbrook Residence

John Thurston Clark Memorial Building
(503 Queen Street)

Construction of this large, well-built building on the corner of Queen and Carleton streets began in 1879. In that year the first floor and basement were built with walls two feet thick. The second and third floors were added in 1880-1881. The building shows the influence of the Second Empire Revival style, which can also be seen in other downtown buildings such as the Randolph Building, the Neil Building and City Hall, and it is typical of federal government buildings designed at that time. Built on land which had been part of the Military Compound, it was used as a post office and customs house until 1915, when a new post office was constructed between it and the Officers' Quarters. In 1950 the federal government gave the old building to the province, and the customs house and other federal offices were moved in 1951 to a new federal building. Various provincial departments and agencies then occupied the old post office until it officially opened as the John Thurston Clark Memorial Library in September 1960.

John Thurston Clark, who died in 1921 from injuries suffered during World War I, was the son of the Hon. William G. Clark, a distinguished Fredericton businessman and lieutenant-governor from 1940 to 1945. At his death in 1948 Mr. Clark left the city a large sum of money for the purchase of a building to provide permanent quarters for the York-Sunbury Historical Society and a "reading room" for young people. The Lemont Building on Campbell Street was purchased and became the city's first public library. In January 1955 it was dedicated to the memory of Mr. Clark's son. Within five years the library had run out of space; an agreement was signed in April 1960 whereby the province gave the city the old post office in exchange for the Lemont Building. In October 1971 the building was extensively damaged by a fire which destroyed approximately 45,000 books. A new library was constructed, and the city considered demolishing the building. There was opposition from the Military Compound Board, which recommended that it be preserved. The province agreed, assumed ownership of the building, and restored it in 1973. The National Exhibition Centre occupied part of the building in 1976 and was joined in 1977 by the New Brunswick Sports Hall of Fame, which had been established in 1970. The National Exhibition Centre closed in 1997, and the Sports Hall of Fame now occupies the whole building. It contains memorabilia and portraits of all members of the hall, including boxer Yvon Durelle, hockey stars Gordie Drillon, Willie O'Ree and Danny Grant, jockey Ron Turcotte, and golfers Mabel Thompson and Mary Ann Driscoll.

The building on the left in the painting is the Men's Barracks, one of the four early military buildings still standing in the Military Compound.

JOHN THURSTON CLARK MEMORIAL BUILDING

The Military Compound

(Queen Street)

Officers' Quarters

The military has had a strong presence in Fredericton from the time the site was chosen as the capital of the province in 1785. When the city was first laid out and surveyed, all the land between Queen Street and the river and between Regent Street and Carleton Street was reserved for the military. Between 1784 and 1869, British soldiers in "scarlet tunics with pipe-clayed helmets and belts and white gloves" were stationed here and were a common site on Fredericton streets. For many years they acted as a fire service for Fredericton and helped civil power with duties such as breaking up unruly crowds at elections. The military constructed a number of buildings within the compound, and after the British soldiers left in 1869, these buildings were put to other use. In 1883, the federal government set up "A" Company of the Canadian Infantry School, which occupied the compound until 1920. Only four of the old military buildings are still standing: the Officers' Quarters, the Guard House, the Men's Barracks and the Military Arms Stores.

The Mens' Barracks, a long stone building the end of which can be seen in the painting of the John Thurston Clark Memorial Building, was completed in 1828 to replace an older wooden barracks. The new three-storey building could house two hundred soldiers in the upper floors; cannon, ammunition and equipment were stored below.

After the British soldiers left, the building was used for a time as a Temperance Hall. When the Canadian Infantry School left, it became a warehouse for the New Brunswick Liquor Control Board. It was later taken over by the Military Compound Board and renovated by 1977. One room was restored to its state in the 1860s, while the rest of the building became offices for Historical Resources and the Provincial Archaeological Branch. When an adjacent building was torn down in the 1980s, a sundial was uncovered high on the east wall.

The Officers' Quarters, which now houses the York-Sunbury Museum, was once both smaller and larger than the building we see today. The original part, the river end, was begun in 1839, while the second part, extending toward Queen Street, was built around 1851; both replaced sections of an earlier wooden barracks, the remains of which are now outlined only by the foundation. The eleven cast iron pillars which support the present veranda were brought from England, while the stone came from a local quarry. Drill inspections, garden parties, skating parties, tennis parties, cricket matches and regular band concerts took place in the area around the barracks and were part of the social life of Fredericton for over a century. Other less pleasant things took place in the area as well. The river end of the Officers' Quarters is said to have been the site of military executions, and soldiers were frequently flogged in the compound for less serious offences.

OFFICERS' QUARTERS

Guard House

The smallest of the military buildings still existing is the stone Guard House, which was built in 1828. It originally had seven windowless cells, which were very cold in the winter. After City Hall burned in 1875, it became the city police office and lockup until 1881. It was used for storage after this until it was restored in 1971. Next to the Guard House is a small wooden building which was built around 1832 and first used as a military stores building. Around 1885 it was enlarged and used for a time as a military hospital. It later became a residence for the caretaker of the armoury. Since 1990 it has been the home of Downtown Development, Inc.

GUARD HOUSE

Government House

(Woodstock Road)

Government House stands on a site which has considerable historic significance. It was first occupied by the Wolustukwiyik and later by the Acadians long before the first English-speaking settlers arrived. The site also contains an old burial ground which was used by both Wolustukwiyik and Acadians. In 1785 Governor Thomas Carleton purchased this land and constructed a large wooden building, which was called Mansion House. In 1816, many years after he had left the province, the provincial government purchased both the house and the surrounding fifty acres as the official residence for future lieutenant-governors. When Sir Howard Douglas was appointed in 1824, he was not impressed with the building, which had been neglected for years; it did not seem suitable for housing a lieutenant-governor. His problems with the house were solved the next year when the building was destroyed in a fire believed to have been deliberately set. Douglas therefore rented the Edgecombe House on King Street as a temporary residence, and a year later, in 1826, the Council agreed to provide funds for the construction of a new Government House on the site of the old Mansion House.

The new building was designed by Barrack Master J.E. Woolford, who also designed King's College. The cornerstone was laid 1 July 1826, and the walls were constructed from local sandstone quarried on the Hanwell Road. Upon completion it was the largest house in Fredericton. Its fifty-two rooms provided spacious accommodations for the lieutenant-governor and his family and servants, as well as ample space for entertaining and doing government business. Some felt it was far more impressive than the governors' residences in Quebec and York. Others considered it an offence to good taste and good architectural design.

Sir John Harvey, who was lieutenant-governor from 1837 to 1841, lived here "in greater splendour than any succeeding lieutenant-governor, his progress to Church always being a most gorgeous affair, with soldiers and military band, state carriage and magnificence of all descriptions." He was also said to have given three dinners a week and a ball every fortnight.

Successive lieutenant-governors lived here until 1890, when Sir Leonard Tilley was appointed to a second term. He refused to continue living here, since he felt the government allowance for maintaining it was inadequate. He decided to reside in Saint John, coming to Fredericton only when the Assembly was in session or when he was needed. Premier Andrew Blair's government therefore decided no further appropriations would be made for the upkeep of the building, and from 1890 until 1974 New Brunswick had no official residence for the lieutenant-governor. Those appointed to the office lived at home or rented premises in Fredericton when the Assembly was in session.

The building now called Old Government House was vacant until occupied by the Deaf and Dumb Institute from 1897 to 1903. It was then closed until purchased in 1919 by the federal government for use by the Military Hospitals Commission as a hospital and rest home for returning veterans. By 1922 it was virtually deserted; gradually it was vandalized and the gardens destroyed. It remained neglected until 1932, when it was taken over by the Royal Canadian Mounted Police as the headquarters for "J" Division. With the opening of the new RCMP headquarters on Regent Street in 1990, it was again abandoned. It has since been presented to the province and is at present being restored to serve its old function as Government House, the residence and offices of the lieutenant-governor.

GOVERNMENT HOUSE

The Justice Building
(423 Queen Street)

What is now the provincial Justice Building started its life as the provincial Normal School. The first school for training teachers was constructed in 1848 on the corner of King and Regent streets. It burned in 1850, and for a time all teacher training took place in Saint John. In 1870 the government decided to concentrate all teacher training in Fredericton. For a time this took place in the Men's Barracks, which had recently been vacated when the British soldiers were withdrawn. This building proved to be unsuitable, since it was damp and cold and could not be used efficiently as a school without major renovations. Nor could it accommodate enough students to fill the demand for teachers. As a result construction of a new building began in 1876 on a site within the Military Compound that had once been occupied by a hospital. The building, referred to as the Normal School, opened in 1877 and was used until it was partially destroyed by fire in 1929. Two years later, in 1931, a new and larger brick Normal School was opened, which was described as "the power house of our system of education." Constructed partly on the remains of the old Normal School, the new building retained the Gothic arches in the front porch, while the back section, built in 1914, is designed differently.

In 1947 the building became Teachers' College; all teacher training in the province continued to be carried on here until 1965, when the college moved to a new building on the campus of the University of New Brunswick. For a time the building was part of Fredericton's high school system, which was overcrowded. When the new high school opened on Prospect Street in 1972, the city planned to demolish the building, but because of strong opposition from citizens the province took it over, remodelled it to house the law courts and offices, and renamed it the Justice Building.

The Justice Building

York County Jail

(668 Brunswick Street)

There have been three York County jails constructed in Fredericton. The first, built shortly after the Loyalists arrived, was a small building made of squared timbers bolted together; it stood between the road and the river at the foot of Forest Hill. It was replaced in 1800 by a building constructed on the east side of Regent Street between King and Brunswick streets; it had a yard in which prisoners sentenced to hard labour could be put to work breaking rock. At this time it was common practice to confine the mentally ill or "lunatics" to the jail, and they, along with vagrants and debtors, made up most of the inmates. A House of Correction was established in York County in 1830 for those sentenced to hard labour, and the first Lunatic Asylum opened in Saint John in 1836. This took some of the pressure off the jail and allowed the magistrates to sell some of the surrounding land and to use the proceeds to construct a more suitable jail. Four lots east of York Street, between Brunswick and George, containing one acre of land, were purchased in January 1840 as a site for the new building.

This building was designed by J.E. Woolford, who had earlier designed King's College and Government House. Seventy five feet long and fifty feet wide, it was built of granite blocks fifteen inches wide and three feet long. Some field stone was mixed in with the granite on the back wall. The outside walls, forty inches thick, are actually two walls with an air space in between. It is not clear when construction was completed, but the building was in use in 1843. The jail had a basement, a first and second floor, and an attic. The jailer originally lived in the basement, which also had two small windowless dungeons, used on rare occasions. It was a bread-and-water prison, lighted by candles and heated only by the basement fireplace. It housed both criminals and debtors, who were kept in jail until they could find a way to discharge their debts. Over the years it was modernized, but by the 1970s it was considered unsuitable by modern standards, and there were a number of escapes. It was finally closed in 1997.

York County Jail

York County Court House
(635 Queen Street)

This brick building, built in 1855-1856, stands on the site of the first Market House in Fredericton, erected by James Taylor in 1815. Taylor had constructed the building under a license from the Governor-in-Council approving its use as a town market. The York County magistrates held their sessions in the upper storey of the building, which they rented from Taylor until 1817 and then purchased, having decided it would be suitable for a court house. The Justices of the Peace were then given title to the land by the province but were warned not to allow "any Tavern, Inn, or Ale house to be kept in any part of the present or other building or buildings erected, or to be erected, on the land," or at any time "to permit Rum, brandy, gin, or any other strong liquor to be sold" in the building or any other buildings constructed on the site. Failure to abide by these rules would see the land revert to the Crown.

After a fire in 1825, which destroyed over fifty buildings in Fredericton, the National School needed a home, and the second storey of the old Market House was used for a time. By 1853 the building had deteriorated to such an extent that the magistrates decided to tear it down and build a new one. According to the editor of the *Royal Gazette*, "It was high time. The thing which at present bears the name is not fit even for the Butcher's shambles which occupy its lower storey."

Construction began on a new building in 1855 under the supervision of a committee chaired by Robert Gowan, the chief draughtsman of the Crown land office, and the building was completed in 1856. It, too, served as both Market House and Court House, and its "flat planes . . . relieved only by decorative stone finishing" made it a much-admired piece of architecture. In 1882 the market was moved to City Hall, and the lower portion of the Court House became the County Record Office. Renovations done in the 1950s added the glass blocks which have inspired the comment that the Court House is now "more utilitarian than aesthetically pleasing."

York County Court House

City Hall

(397 Queen Street)

The present City Hall is the fourth building on this site in Phoenix Square, which received its name because of the many fires that resulted in new buildings constantly rising from the ashes. The first building was know as the Tank House. It was built in 1822 by a group of citizens who obtained permission from the governor to dig a tank or well in Phoenix Square and to erect over it a building to prevent the water freezing and to house the hand-operated fire engine. This two-storey building was completed in 1823. In 1828 the Union Fire Club added a fire bell to the cupola. In 1848, when the city was incorporated, a second market place was proposed for this site, which was opposed by those who supported the market in the Court House further down Queen Street. Others wanted to see the old Tank House removed. The problem was solved in September 1850, when the Tank House burned to the ground in a fire believed to have been no accident.

A new building with two floors and no basement, said to be more a Market House than a place "to conduct the city's business," was quickly constructed. The first floor housed a market and the second the York Division 2 of the Sons of Temperance. Shortly after this a basement was built under the building by a local butcher, who was allowed to operate a shop there for a dollar a year. He rented part of this space for use as a grocery and liquor store, an unusual tenant for a building referred to as the Tem-perance Hall. This building burned in May 1867, and again arson was suspected.

Its disappearance paved the way for a new combined city hall and market. This three-storey building had a market in the basement, a council room and offices for the mayor and other city officials on the second floor, and a large auditorium or City Hall on the third floor, which could hold some eight hundred people and was used for meetings and entertainments. This building was considered ugly by some people, since it was a plain rectangular building with no decorations and nothing to show it was City Hall. Eight years later, in 1875, it, too, was destroyed by fire.

Council decided immediately to rebuild on the same site, and the new City Hall, which is still in use today, was completed in October 1876. This was a much more elaborate building of brick and stone, described as "Gothic of the Venetian type," with its front porch and tower over the main door and its sunken panel bearing the coat of arms of the city. The building originally measured one hundred and fifteen feet long and sixty feet wide. The basement, designed as a market, originally had four entrances. It also contained the city magistrate's office and cells. The first floor held offices and the council chamber, and upstairs was a public hall or theatre with 810 seats. Referred to as the Opera House, for the next sixty or more years it was the entertainment centre of Fredericton.

The tower, which is 115 feet high, was originally supposed to house a fire bell, but the plans were altered and the tower strengthened to bear the weight of a large clock, which was added in 1878. It was presented to the city by Mayor George Fenety, who was also responsible for the construction of the fountain in front of City Hall. Originally the fountain was more elaborate than it appears today, with three basins. The top basin had to be removed because of complaints from ladies that the wind sprinkled water on them while they were on their way to the Opera House. The second basin was also removed, and now there is only one. "Freddie the Fountain Boy," more commonly known today as "Freddie the little nude dude," has directed the spray at the top of the fountain since Mayor Fenety's day, but the Freddie you see outside is a replica of the original, now kept indoors for his own safety.

In 1940 the Opera House closed and the theatre was converted into office space, which included a new council chamber. The farmers' market moved out to the square, where it continued to operate until the Boyce Farmers' Market opened in 1952. In 1975 construction began on an addition designed to be as compatible as possible with the old building, which was changed very little.

CITY HALL

COURTESY OF ANNE AND BRAD WOODSIDE

St. Dunstan's School

(327 Regent Street)

Many of the schools established in New Brunswick in the nineteenth century were controlled by religious groups. When the original St. Dunstan's Church was constructed in 1845, the Roman Catholics established their first school in their old chapel, which had been constructed in 1824. They moved it to the back of the church lot on Regent Street and used it as a church hall and school until a larger church hall was constructed in 1887. The children were taught by members of the Sisters of Charity, who had come to Fredericton in 1858. By the early 1900s the space was not sufficient for the number of children in the parish, and in 1910 St. Dunstan's School was built to accommodate them. It was constructed on the site of the old Roman Catholic cemetery on Regent Street. For many years the majority of students were Roman Catholics, but the school eventually became a neighbourhood school attended by students of various faiths. The Sisters of Charity continued to share teaching duties in the school until the 1970s. The building is still owned by St. Dunstan's parish and is leased to School District 18.

ST. DUNSTAN'S SCHOOL

COURTESY OF LAURA POYATOS

ℬOLDON'S ℱOOD ⓈTORE *and* ℱHE ℱOWLER ℋOUSE

(279 and 289 Regent)

The land on which these two buildings stand was once part of the seventy-two-acre estate of the Hon. George Sproule, the province's first Surveyor General. The land on either side of what became Needham Street was sold in 1829 to two Saint John merchants. It was sold again in 1838 to John T. Lawrence, a carpenter. He lived in an old house which, after many alterations, became the front part of Hogan's Food Store, now Bolden's Food Store, a popular breakfast and lunch stop for many Frederictonians. The land on the opposite side of Needham Street had a house on it by 1859, when it was purchased by William "Moosehorn" Fowler, who was in the lumber business and was secretary of the Fredericton Boom Company. The Fowler family lived in this attractive red house for approximately one hundred years. It was sold in 1960 to Leycester D'Arcy, QC, who still resides here.

COURTESY OF CAROL AND WILLIAM SPRAY

BOLDEN'S FOOD STORE AND THE FOWLER HOUSE

CLARK BUILDING

(300 King Street)

This large brick building on the corner of York and King streets was for many years the home of J. Clark and Sons. The company was founded in 1883 by John T. Clark when he and his son, W.G. Clark, took over T. Johnston and Co., a farm machinery and carriage business in Saint John. They immediately moved the business to Fredericton, first establishing themselves on the corner of York and Queen streets before moving their operations to King Street in 1894. They soon needed more space, and this new building was constructed in 1899. The company's success was assured soon after the arrival of the automobile; in 1915, they established the first Chevrolet dealership in Canada. The dealership moved to Prospect Street in 1973, but this building is still owned by the Clark family.

CLARK BUILDING

Neil Building

(384 Queen Street)

This painting shows a number of nineteenth-century commercial buildings on the south side of Queen Street. The large brick building in the centre is the Neil Building, which was constructed in 1894 for J.S. Neil and Sons. This was a large hardware business founded in 1838 by John Neil, a Scot, who also owned a large farm on the north side of the Saint John River. In 1854 John Neil was responsible for introducing the sport of curing when he imported the first curling stones to the city. These caused some confusion for customs officials, who had no idea what they were. John's son, James S. Neil, later took over the business. For a time Fredericton's first radio station operated out of this building.

NEIL BUILDING

Randolph Building or Old Gleaner Building

(371 Queen Street)

This building was constructed by Archibald Fitz Randolph in 1878 on the west side of Phoenix Square. It replaced a smaller square brick building which, in 1869, had housed Guiou's Cheap Store. The new building was designed to complement the new City Hall, which had been constructed in 1876 and which Randolph admired. He was president of the People's Bank and the owner of a lumber business, and in his new building he established the city's first wholesale grocery business. For many years it was the largest business of its kind in Fredericton. After Randolph left for California in 1896, the building was used continuously as a store and offices until 1959, when the *Fredericton Daily Gleaner* moved there from an old wooden building further down Queen Street, opposite the Military Compound. The *Gleaner* had originated in Chatham, where it began publication in 1829. It was purchased by James H. Crockett in 1880 and moved to Fredericton in 1884, and by 1951 it had outgrown its original home. In the Randolph Building, the papers were printed, carried from the press to the mailing room where advertisements were inserted, and counted and bundled; then the drivers had to carry them out to their trucks for delivery. All this took four hours if all went well. By the 1970s the building was no longer suitable for the efficient production of a newspaper, and in 1980 the *Gleaner* moved to new quarters with conveyer belts and modern machinery. The Old Gleaner Building now contains offices.

RANDOLPH BUILDING OR OLD GLEANER BUILDING

Legislative Building

(706 Queen Street)

In the 1870s the Legislative Assembly was still meeting in the old Province Hall, which had been built in 1802. Since the 1820s people had been complaining that Province Hall was small and plain and "too low to make a good appearance." By the 1870s it was considered an eyesore, and a new building was in the planning stages when, in 1880, a fire completely destroyed one wing of the old building. With the blight on the landscape no longer functional, some people in Saint John began immediately to agitate for a new Legislative Assembly to be constructed there, not in Fredericton. This stirred up Frederictonians, and the House of Assembly quickly met and decided to tear down the rest of the building and construct a new building on the same site.

The building was designed by J.C. Dumaresq, a Nova Scotian architect, and the contractor was William Lawlor, of Chatham. The stone came from Dorchester by schooner; its arrival and the unloading of the big blocks attracted large crowds, who watched as the blocks of stone were hand-cut before they were set in place. At one time the project employed sixty-five stone-cutters and their labourers, sixty-five masons and their labourers, fifteen carpenters, six iron workers and two blacksmiths.

The new Legislative Assembly was built in the Second Empire Style, a combination of Gothic and Classical forms used to build mansions and palaces in seventeenth-century France. The revival version of this style was considered suitable for large government buildings in the late nineteenth century. Some newspaper writers called the style "Corinthian," with its pillars, its mansard roof, and its 135-foot-high dome. Far above, and dominating the portico, is a six-foot image of Britannia holding a trident, and around the columns or pillars of the portico are sixteen carved heads. The statue and sixteen heads were the work of James McAvity, a well-known stone cutter from Portland, who also carved the coat of arms for City Hall. Inside the building is a grand spiral staircase which winds its way up to the first and second floors.

According to the newspapers, no provision was made for a cornerstone, "the Executive having come to the conclusion that it would be more suitable to put a Memorial Stone in the Legislative Library." The builder, Mr. Lawlor, had other ideas, and he decided to lay "a contractor's stone," which was placed at the base of one of the columns of the portico and laid "with all due care and regardless of formalities." The building was officially opened in 1882 with a "Ball and Promenade Concert," to which nearly fifteen hundred ladies were admitted free of charge, while gentlemen had to pay. The ball began at eight-thirty in the evening. Two bands played, one upstairs and one downstairs, and a late supper was served in the Legislative Library at the back of the building. Today, the Legislative

LEGISLATIVE BUILDING

Library contains over 50,000 volumes, including a 1783 copy of the *Domesday Book* and a complete set of engravings of *The Birds of America* by John James Audubon.

One of the most impressive parts of the building is the throne or speaker's chair — considered a throne when the lieutenant-governor, the Queen's representative, is in attendance and the seat of the Speaker of the House when the Assembly is in session. This throne and the clerk's table and desk were saved from the old Province Hall when it burned. Also saved from the old building and now hanging in the Assembly Chamber are large portraits of George III and Queen Charlotte, which had been brought from England by Col. Edward Winslow in 1806.

Standing beside the Legislative Assembly is a modest stone building which was erected in 1816 as an office for Provincial Secretary William F. Odell. Originally it was only one storey high, but a second storey and attic were added between 1867 and 1870 to provide more offices and storage space. This building, with its old-time locks, bell pulls, recessed fireplaces and narrow stairways, is the oldest surviving public building in Fredericton.

Legislative Assembly from King Street